Allergies

Dr. Alvin Silverstein,

Virginia Silverstein, and

Laura Silverstein Nunn

My Health

Franklin Watts

A Division of Grolier Publishing

New York • London • Hong Kong • Sydney

Danbury, Connecticut

Photographs©: Stock Shop/Medicrome/Anatomyworks: 29 (Marcia Hartsock); Envision: 17 (George Mattei); Photo Researchers: 28 (Scott Camazine), 34 (Mark Clarke/SPL), 19 right (John Durham/SPL), 20 (Ralph C. Eagle), 21 left (R. J. Erwin), 16 (Dr. Brian Eyden/SPL), 15 (Eric V. Grave), 9 (Eddy Gray/SPL), 27 (Phillip Hayson), 32 bottom (J. F. Wilson), 37 (Susan Leavines), 4, 30 (Damien Lovegrove/SPL), 7, 10, 11 (Dr. P. Marazzi/SPL), 13, 23 bottom (Oliver Meckes/Ottawa), 23 right (Microfield Scientific/SPL), 23 top (Sidney Moulds/SPL), 19 left (Secchi, Lecaque, Roussel, UCLAF, CNRI/SPL), 32 top (SIU), 25 (Andrew Syred/SPL), 26 (Jeanne White), 21 right (Jim Zipp)

Medical illustration by Leonard Morgan.
Cartoons by Rick Stromoski.

Visit Franklin Watts on the Internet at:
http://publishing.grolier.com

Library of Congress Cataloging-in-Publication Data

Silverstein, Alvin.
　　Allergies / by Alvin Silverstein, Virginia Silverstein, and Laura Silverstein Nunn.
　　　　p.　cm.—(My Health)
　　Includes bibliographical references and index.
　　Summary: Discusses the nature and effects of allergies, who gets them, how they develop, the different kinds, and how they are treated.
　　ISBN 0-531-11581-X (lib.bdg.)　　0-531-16409-8 (pbk.)
　　1. Allergy—Juvenile literature.　[1. Allergy] I. Silverstein, Virginia B. II. Nunn, Laura Silverstein. III. Title. IV. Series: Silverstein, Alvin. My health.
RC585.S53　　1999
616.97—dc21
　　　　　　　　　　　　　　　　　　　　　　　　　　　　　　98-26033
　　　　　　　　　　　　　　　　　　　　　　　　　　　　　　CIP
　　　　　　　　　　　　　　　　　　　　　　　　　　　　　　AC

GROLIER
PUBLISHING

Contents

Itch, Sniffle, and Sneeze

Do you sneeze every summer? Do you get itchy bumps on your skin when you eat a chocolate bar? Do you have trouble breathing if you play with a puppy? If you have problems like these, you may have an *allergy*.

Allergies are unusual reactions to things in the world around us. Most people can eat a chocolate bar without getting bumps on their skin. Most people can breathe in the summer air without sneezing. For most people, playing with a puppy is harmless fun. But certain foods, drugs, animal hair and skin—or even the air they breathe—can be like poison for people with allergies.

Did You Know...

About 50 million people in the United States have allergies. That means one out of every five people is allergic to something.

◀ **Some people sneeze when they breathe in pollen from grasses or flowers.**

Most allergic reactions are just plain annoying—itching, sneezing, coughing, watery eyes, and runny nose. But sometimes, allergies can cause serious and even deadly reactions. Fortunately, most people do not have severe allergic reactions. But they may miss many days of school or work because of allergies.

What causes allergies? Do you have any allergies? What can you do to stop the itch, sniffle, and sneeze? Let's find out more about them.

Did You Know...

Humans aren't the only animals that can have allergies. Your dog or cat can get allergies too.

AACHOO!

Who Gets Allergies?

Anybody can get allergies—boy or girl, young or old. Kids usually have more allergies than adults, but the first allergic reaction can happen at any age. Even babies can have allergies. Some babies may become allergic to cow's milk or certain foods if they are given them too early. Kids who are exposed to cigarette smoke are more likely to develop allergies.

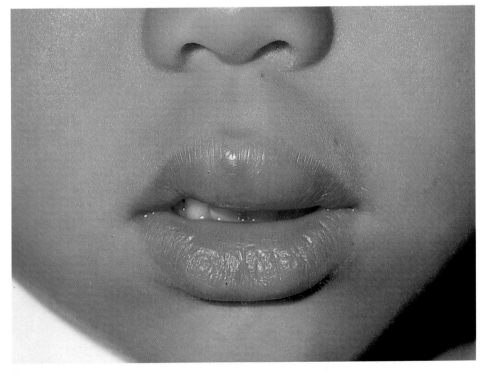

This boy's upper lip is swollen because he had an allergic reaction after eating peanuts.

You cannot catch allergies from your friends the way you can catch a cold. Allergies tend to run in families. If your mom or dad has allergies, then you have a 20 to 50 percent chance of getting some type of allergy too. If both your parents have allergies, then you have a 40 to 75 percent chance of getting allergies. If neither of them has allergies, the chances of your being allergic drop to between 5 and 15 percent.

A Whole New Generation of Allergy Sufferers

Many years ago, people thought the cure for allergies was to move to the Southwest, where there was no ragweed pollen, no freshly cut grasses, no pollen-producing trees, and no mold. In the desert, in places like Tucson, Arizona, there was just clear air, cactus, and sunshine. No more sneezing, no more sniffling!

In the 1940s, Tucson had a population of 20,000 people. Now, 500,000 people live there—and half of them suffer from hay fever or asthma. Why? Because when the allergy sufferers moved to Tucson many years ago, they brought things from home with them, like mulberry trees and Bermuda grass. And because allergies run in families, the new settlers gave birth to a whole new generation of allergy sufferers, who now live in a place with plenty to sneeze at.

What Are Allergies?

An allergy is an unusual reaction to a substance that is usually considered harmless. A substance that causes an allergic reaction is called an **allergen.**

An allergen may get into your body when you breathe it in, eat it, or when it is injected into your skin.

Some common allergens that we breathe in include **pollens** (tiny powdery particles flowers use to make

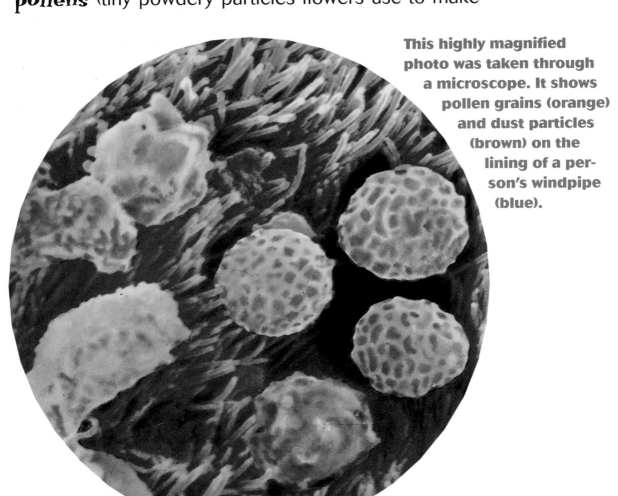

This highly magnified photo was taken through a microscope. It shows pollen grains (orange) and dust particles (brown) on the lining of a person's windpipe (blue).

Can You Outgrow Allergies?

Allergies can change as the years go by. When you get older, you may get a new allergy that you did not have when you were young. Some allergy symptoms may disappear, while others may get worse. For instance, many babies and young children who get an allergic skin rash called **eczema** outgrow it. But many kids with eczema get other allergies when they are older.

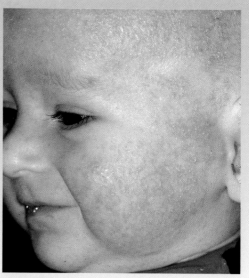

The rash on this baby's face and head is eczema.

seeds), molds, and dust. Allergens that we eat or drink include foods, such as milk and peanuts, and drugs, such as penicillin. The poisons in insect and bee stings can act as allergens, too.

Allergies can affect different parts of the body: eyes, nose, head, stomach, skin, throat, and lungs. Allergens that are breathed in often cause a stuffed-up, runny nose. They may also cause sneezing, coughing, watery eyes, a scratchy throat, and breathing problems. Allergens that touch the skin may produce itchy rashes or itchy bumps called **hives.** People with allergies may get headaches and stomachaches too.

Different people can have a different reaction to the same allergen. For instance, eating peanuts may cause a rash in one person, a stomachache in another person, and breathing problems in a third person.

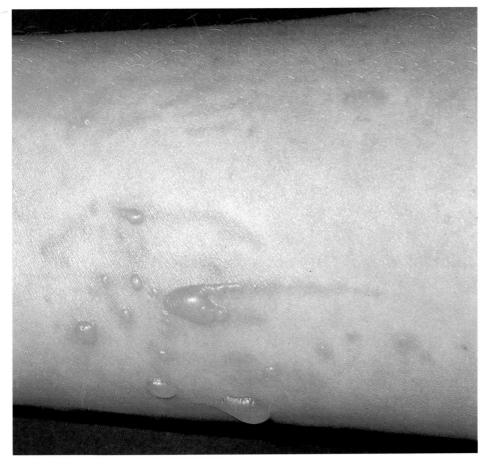

This blistery red rash was caused by an allergy to seaweed, which touched the skin of a swimmer's arm.

How Do We Get Allergies?

People often get sick when tiny germs invade their bodies, multiply, and produce poisons. The human body has many defenses against germs. It has a whole army of soldiers that fight for us—our **white blood cells**. They are part of our **immune system.** White blood cells are always on guard, swimming through the blood and even squeezing through the spaces between body cells.

The main job of some white blood cells is to spot foreign invaders, such as disease germs that can make us sick. These white blood cells send out chemical signals to call in the germ fighters. Some of them go after the germs and gobble them up. Others make proteins called **antibodies,** which are like ammunition for the white cell soldiers. These special proteins may damage the germs or make it easier for the white blood cells to catch and kill the invaders.

After the battle is over, some of the antibodies stay in the body. If the same kind of germs invade again, those antibodies will quickly make a whole

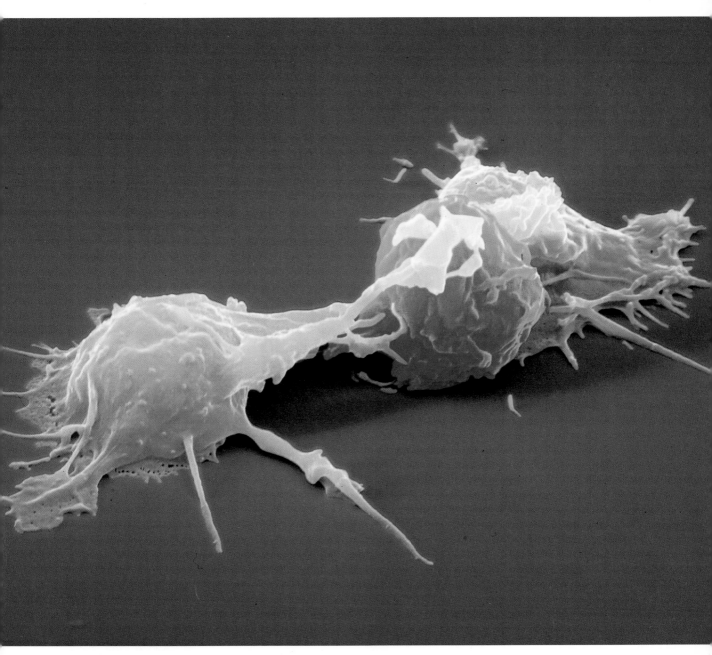

The immune system helps protect us from diseases. Here white blood cells are attacking a cancerous leukemia cell.

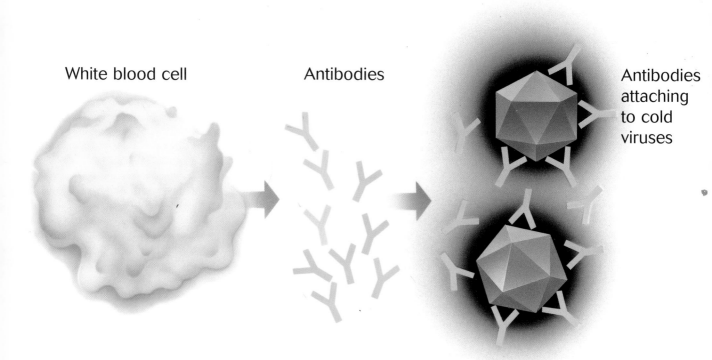

White blood cell

Antibodies

Antibodies attaching to cold viruses

When germs, such as viruses, invade your body, some white blood cells produce antibodies. The antibodies attach to the germ and help destroy it.

new supply of ammunition to fight the germs. As a result, the person will not get sick. The person is now immune to that illness.

Some people have an immune system that is a little too active. It makes antibodies against chemicals that would not have caused any harm. These may be chemicals on the surface of dust or pollen grains, or chemicals in foods. Drugs such as penicillin can also make the immune system react. The antibodies produced in these kinds of reactions are called **IgEs.** (A different kind of antibodies, called **IgGs,** fight against most disease germs.)

IgEs can be found in various parts of the body—the nose, throat, lungs, stomach, and skin. These antibodies are Y-shaped. The arms of the Y can latch onto allergens. Different IgEs match different kinds of allergens—they fit together like the pieces of a jigsaw puzzle. For instance, a milk allergen fits perfectly with one kind of IgE antibody, while a grass pollen allergen fits together with another type of IgE antibody.

Unemployed Antibodies

The proper targets for IgE antibodies are **parasites,** such as the pinworms that can live in people's intestines. Some medical experts believe that more people have allergies today because our living conditions are cleaner, and therefore internal parasites are rare in developed countries. Now that the IgE's number-one enemy is gone, it has been left with nothing to do except cause trouble.

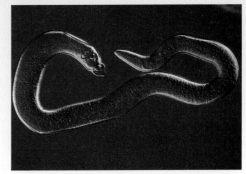

IgE antibodies are supposed to fight parasites like this trichina worm.

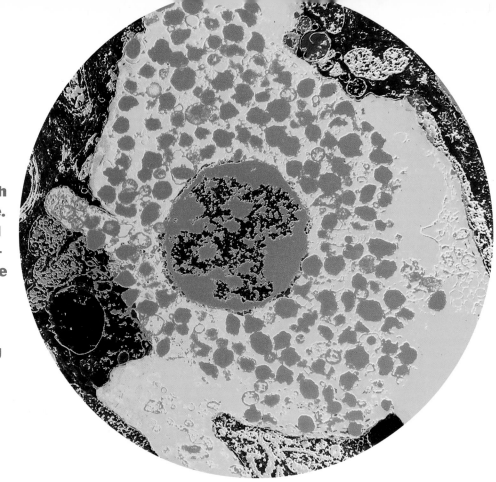

This highly-magnified photo of a mast cell was taken through a microscope. The small red granules contain histamine and other chemicals that can produce swelling and itching.

The "foot" of the IgE's Y-shape can attach to **mast cells** in many parts of your body—your skin, the lining of your nose, your stomach, your throat, or your lungs. The trouble starts when IgEs attached to mast cells grab hold of allergens.

The first time you are exposed to an allergen, you may not have any allergy symptoms at all. For instance, if you eat a strawberry, your body may mistake it for an invader and produce IgE antibodies, but there won't be enough of them to bother you.

The next time you eat strawberries, your body produces more IgEs. The more strawberries you eat, the worse your allergy symptoms will become. This kind of exposure build-up is called **sensitization.** Your body has now become sensitive to strawberries and will have an allergic reaction, like an itchy rash or a stomachache, every time you eat them. This process may not happen all in one day. It can take weeks, months, or even years to develop an allergy.

Some people are allergic to strawberries.

What Happens During an Allergy Attack?

Picture a pollen grain floating through the air. It is tiny—too small to see without a microscope. You breathe in the pollen grain and it settles into the lining of your nose. The watery **mucus** in your nose starts to break down the pollen grain, freeing its chemicals. If you are sensitized to that kind of pollen, the IgE antibodies that are attached to mast cells in your nose grab the pollen chemicals and hold them tight. The mast cells then send out a chemical called **histamine.**

Histamine's job is to help fight invaders. It produces **inflammation,** making body cells swollen and watery. That's why your nose and eyes may start to run when you breathe in pollen grains, or dust, or molds. (If you are stung by a bee or touch poison ivy, histamine sent out by the mast cells in the skin causes swelling or rashes.) White blood cells can move

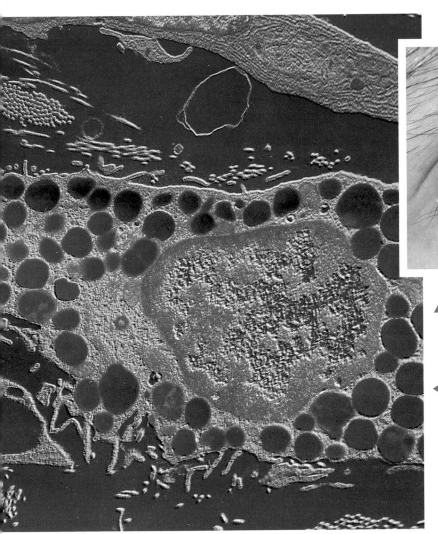

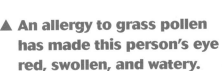

▲ An allergy to grass pollen has made this person's eye red, swollen, and watery.

◄ During an allergic reaction, granules in sensitized mast cells spill out chemicals that produce swelling and itching.

more easily through inflamed cells. So if germs were invading, inflammation would be a good thing. But a reaction to a harmless allergen just makes you feel miserable.

Kinds of Allergies

One of the most common types of allergies is **hay fever**. Hay fever feels like you have a cold. You sniffle and sneeze, and your nose runs. But hay fever comes at the same time every year. And, unlike colds, it isn't caused by germs. It is caused by an allergy.

Most people with hay fever are allergic to pollen from plants, especially **ragweed** pollen. Plants need

An Explosion of Pollen

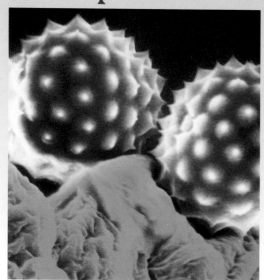

One ragweed plant can make 8 billion pollen grains! If you sat down and made dots on a paper all day and all night (even in your sleep), it would take you about 25 years to make 8 billion dots. But a ragweed plant can make 8 billion pollen grains in just a month.

This photo of ragweed pollen was taken through a microscope. The technicians who process these photos often add bright colors to make objects easier to see.

Pollen blowing from a pine cone (left) and timothy grass (top)

pollen to make seeds, which grow into new plants. To make new plants, the pollen must get from one plant to another. Plants with sweet-smelling, colorful flowers are pollinated by insects, and they do not usually cause allergies. But the pollen of ragweed, grasses, and many trees is very light, and it rides the winds to get to other plants. Winds can carry pollen very long distances.

Not everybody with hay fever sneezes at the same time of the year. Different people are allergic to different kinds of pollen. Some get hay fever in the early spring, when the trees are blooming. Others are allergic to grasses that bloom in May or June. Still others are allergic to plants that bloom in the late summer.

Some people are allergic to **molds.** Molds are tiny creatures that feed on rotting plant or animal matter. Molds are a kind of fungus that can grow almost anywhere, especially in warm, moist places. Have you ever seen mold growing on an old bread crust or on very old food left in the refrigerator? You may be familiar with mildew, the kind of mold that grows on a shower curtain.

Molds make huge numbers of **spores,** which are kind of like seeds. Spores are very tiny—as tiny and light as pollen. Like pollen grains, spores are carried into the air we breathe.

The molds that grow on old bread (top) produce an enormous number of tiny spores that can trigger allergic reactions. When the mold is magnified about 450 times (bottom), it is possible to see its structure. When it is magnified even more (right), it is possible to see individual spores.

Activity 1:
Making a Mushroom Spore Picture

Cut the stalk away from a mushroom close to the cap. Place the cap (flat underside down) on a piece of white or black paper. Put a jar or bowl over the mushroom cap and leave it for several hours. Then carefully remove the bowl and the mushroom cap, and you will see the pattern made by the falling spores. (Like molds, mushrooms are fungi, and they produce billions of tiny spores.) The spore pattern will be just like the pattern of the slits under the mushroom cap.

Did you ever shake out a dusty rag and then sneeze? You may have sneezed because the dust tickled your nose, but some people are actually allergic to **dust.** House dust can be found anywhere—on carpets, bookshelves, curtains, even stuffed toys.

If you put a tiny pile of dust under a microscope, you might be surprised at what you see. House dust may include a variety of things: fibers from bedsheets, flakes of dead skin, pollen grains, pet hair, mold spores, and little bits of insects. Just knowing what is in house dust is enough to make you want to sneeze, but you may actually have to blame your dust allergy on dust mites or, rather, on the poop of **dust mites.** It is so tiny and light that it can easily float through the air, enter your nose, and cause allergy symptoms.

This is a dust mite, magnified to more than 250 times its real size. The dust around it contains hair and fibers.

Even our favorite pets shed dander that can cause allergies.

Have you ever started to sneeze while petting a puppy? You may be allergic to animal **dander**—tiny flakes of skin. Animals shed dander on the carpets and furniture. Different animals have different kinds of dander. So you may be allergic to dogs but not to cats. Or maybe you are fine with cats and dogs, but parakeets make you sneeze.

Pollen, mold spores, dust, and animal dander are all things that you breathe. People may also be allergic to things they eat. If you are allergic to chocolate, for example, you may get a skin rash whenever you eat a candy bar. Some people are allergic to milk, wheat, or eggs. It is not too hard to avoid chocolate, although it might not be much fun. But imagine life without milk and ice cream or spaghetti, bread, and cake.

Lactose Intolerance

More than 50 million Americans feel that they cannot drink milk or other dairy products without having an upset stomach. Many people call this a "milk allergy," but it is not really an allergy, it is a condition called **lactose intolerance**. Milk contains lactose, a milk sugar. Lactose-intolerant people lack an enzyme called lactase, which we need to digest milk products. So when they drink milk or eat ice cream, they may get a stomachache, gas, or diarrhea.

People with lactose intolerance get stomachaches from milk and dairy products. This is not really an allergy.

People can be allergic to medicines, too. Penicillin is a very good drug for killing disease germs, but some people become allergic to it. The first clue that a person is allergic to penicillin is usually a rash. A person who ignores this warning and keeps on taking the drug may get a much worse reaction—or might even die!

Insect bites and bee stings can also cause serious allergies. When a bee or wasp stings you—ouch! That

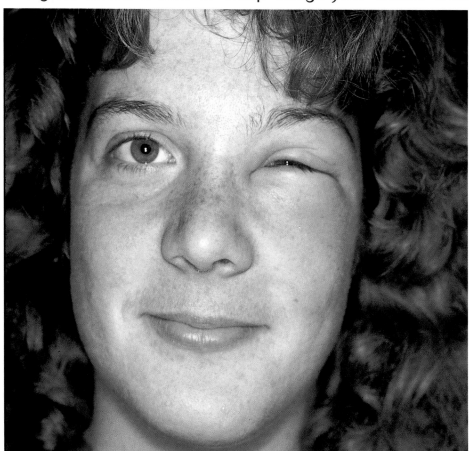

This girl's eye was swollen shut after a bee stung her on the cheek.

really hurts. Your skin gets swollen. This is a normal reaction. But if you are allergic to bee or wasp poison, getting stung could cause a very bad reaction called **anaphylactic shock.** You get hives, big, itchy bumps that pop out all over your body. You feel hot all over. You feel sick to your stomach and throw up. You may have trouble breathing or feel dizzy and faint. You may even pass out and have to be rushed to the hospital. People who know they are allergic to bee stings may carry an injector kit with a drug called **epinephrine,** to use in emergencies.

People may also be allergic to things they touch. Some people are allergic to cotton, wool, or leather in clothing. Other common allergens include detergents, soaps, powders, and perfumes.

Do you know anybody who doesn't get a rash after touching **poison ivy**? Many people have an allergic reaction to the oil of this irritating plant—but not everyone. People usually have to be exposed to poison ivy or other "poison" plants, such as poison oak and poison sumac, more than once before they become sensitive to these plants.

The poison plants: sumac (upper left), ivy (upper right), and oak (bottom).

This girl is using an aerosol inhaler to take a drug that helps control asthma.

Allergies can cause a serious condition called **asthma.** This is a disease in which the airways of the lungs become thick and puffy, and filled with pus. The inflammation prevents air from flowing freely through the airways. People with asthma have difficulty breathing and wheeze as they try to catch a breath.

An asthma attack can be triggered by the same allergens that may cause hay fever or some other allergy. During an asthma attack, mast cells in the lungs release histamine. Asthma attacks can be very frightening and, if they are not treated right away, they can even be fatal.

How Do You Know If You Have Allergies?

You're sneezing and coughing. Your eyes and nose are runny. And your throat is scratchy. Do you have a cold or do you have an allergy? Allergies often occur about the same time every year or they can continue all year long. So if your "cold" never seems to go away, maybe it isn't a cold.

The best way to find out whether you have an allergy or a cold is to see your doctor. He or she will ask you some questions about your symptoms. Then the doctor will test you for allergies. There are two basic kinds of tests: skin tests and blood tests.

Did You Know...

If you have dark rings under your eyes, you may not be getting enough sleep. But those rings might also be a sign of allergies. People with allergies may also have a wrinkle just above the tip of the nose. That comes from rubbing an itchy nose in the typical "allergic salute."

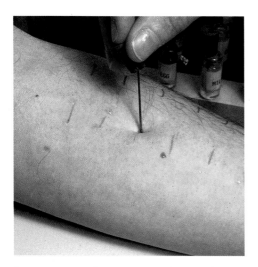

In a scratch test, a person's skin is scratched many times and a different allergen is placed on each scratch.

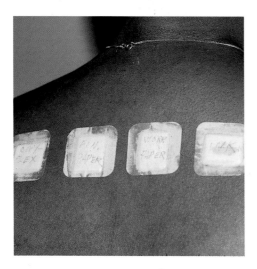

In a patch test, patches containing different allergens are placed against a person's skin.

Skin tests include the **scratch test.** The doctor makes several small scratches on your skin and rubs a different allergen on each scratch. After 15 to 20 minutes, the doctor checks the skin around each scratch. If the skin is red, itchy, or has tiny bumps, you are sensitive to that allergen.

In other skin tests, drops of different allergens are put on your skin. Then, a small needle is used to prick the skin. Or a tiny amount of an allergen solution may be injected right into the skin. The places where you get a rash tell the doctor what you are allergic to.

A special kind of skin test called the **patch test** is used to test people who are allergic to things they touch, such as poison ivy. Doctors cannot use standard tests for this type of allergen because the reaction may not occur for a day or two. Patches that contain the allergen stay on the patient's back for about 48 hours so that the doctor can check for a delayed reaction.

Two main types of blood tests are used to test for allergies. The **RIST test** measures the total amount of IgE in your blood. (High levels of IgE show that you have allergies.) The **RAST test** measures the amounts of specific IgE antibodies in your blood. For instance, if you have an IgE antibody for dust in your blood, then you are probably allergic to house dust.

You can check for food allergies with an **elimination diet.** First you stop eating certain foods for a period of time. Then you try eating the foods one at a time and see if there is any kind of allergic reaction. An even simpler test is to eat a food you suspect you are allergic to and then look for a reaction. But make sure that you have your doctor's okay first—some reactions can be dangerous.

Once you find out whether you have allergies—and if so, which allergens you are sensitive to—you can start a treatment program.

Picky About Peanuts

People who are allergic to peanuts have to be very careful. Even the tiniest amount of peanut can set off a reaction and even lead to anaphylactic shock. These people cannot eat roasted peanuts, candy bars or cake with peanuts, peanut butter, peanut butter cookies, or even potato chips fried in peanut oil. They learn to check the labels of food products and ask about any new food before eating it.

Treating and Preventing Allergies

There is no cure for allergies, but they can be controlled. The only foolproof way to be allergy-free is to avoid the allergens that cause you problems. If you are allergic to a food, you should not eat it. If you are allergic to dust, remove all rugs and curtains from your bedroom and use dustproof covers on your mattress and pillow.

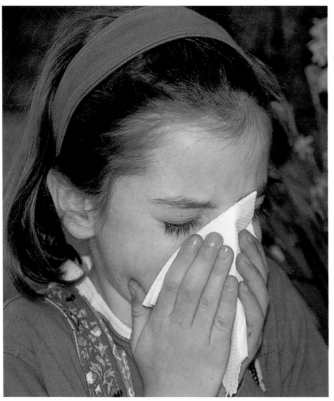

Sometimes, it's not that easy. How can you avoid ragweed when it grows in your neighborhood at certain times of the year? What if a food you are allergic to is hidden in another food, like eggs in a cake or nuts in a candy bar?

It's not always easy, but the miseries of hay fever and other allergies can be prevented or treated.

How to Avoid Allergens

While it is not always easy to avoid the allergens that trigger your allergy attacks, you can lessen your exposure to them. You'd be surprised what an amazing difference it can make in your life. Here are some hints on how you can reduce your exposure:

- Your house should be cleaned thoroughly to get rid of dust mites and mold spores. Remove dust collectors, such as carpets, bookshelves, and stuffed toys, from your home. If that's not possible, keep them clean of allergens.

- Molds that grow on shower curtains can be cleaned with bleach. Moldy food should be thrown out right away.

- Cover your mattresses and pillows with air-tight plastic that keeps out allergens.

- Do not come into contact with animals—even your own pets.

- Stay away from smoking areas because cigarette smoke makes allergies worse.

- Use an air cleaner with a HEPA filter. This device takes allergens out of the air.

- If your allergies come at a certain time of the year, stay indoors. Keep the windows closed so that the pollen and mold spores do not get into your house. Use air-conditioning instead.

When you can't avoid the allergens that bother you, various medical treatments can help keep your allergies under control. These treatments can get rid of allergy symptoms or at least make them milder and easier to handle.

Many people take **antihistamine** drugs to treat their allergies. Remember, histamine is the chemical released by mast cells. It is the main cause of allergy symptoms. An antihistamine stops the harmful effects of histamine.

Decongestants are drugs that reduce swelling in the nasal passages. They help to clear a stopped-up nose so that you can breathe more easily.

Anti-inflammatory drugs also help to reduce inflammation and swelling. They can be used to treat many allergies.

People who have severe allergic reactions need to take a drug called epinephrine. For instance, people who go into anaphylactic shock from bee stings or from a bad reaction to an antibiotic drug are often treated

Did You Know...

Eighteenth-century allergy treatments included a cold water bath to treat hay fever. Like other treatments of the time, it didn't work too well.

with epinephrine. It is also used for people with serious food allergies, such as an allergy to peanuts.

Mast-cell stabilizers are another very effective allergy treatment. Remember that mast cells give off the histamine that gives you an allergic reaction. A mast-cell stabilizer stops the mast cells from releasing histamine and therefore prevents an allergy attack. The most effective mast-cell stabilizer is a nasal spray called Nasalcrom. You can get it over the counter at the drugstore, and medical experts say it is a very safe product.

Many people with asthma carry inhaler devices that deliver drugs called **bronchodilators.** These are drugs that open the airways during an asthma attack. Asthma treatment also includes the regular use of anti-inflammatory drugs to make the airways less sensitive.

Of course, most people with allergies would like to stop allergy attacks before they start. Allergy shots are one way to do this. Each shot contains a tiny amount of an allergen. When it is injected, some of the allergen gets into the blood and causes IgG antibodies to be made. Each injection contains a

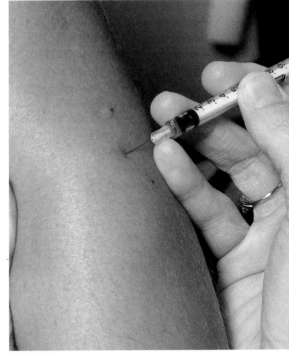

Allergy shots can decrease the body's reactions to allergens.

little more of the allergen, and more IgG to match the antigen is produced. After a while, there is enough of the specific IgG to act as **blocking antibodies.** Then, if you breathe, eat, or touch the allergen, the IgG antibodies will grab it before your IgE allergy antibodies can get to it. Your body is now desensitized to that allergen, and it no longer triggers an allergic reaction.

Activity 2: Allergy Fun on the Internet

If you have a computer with an Internet connection at home or in school, you can find a lot of fun material at the Allerdays web site. There's "Armand's Page," starring an animated Nose. You can read Armand's Diary, watch movies, and e-mail him funny questions. You can also send your own comments and drawings of how allergies affect your life. The address is: http://www.allerdays.com/.

Glossary

allergen—a substance that causes an allergic reaction.

allergy—an overreaction of the immune system to a normally harmless substance, resulting in a rash, sneezing, breathing difficulties, or other symptoms.

anaphylactic shock—a very serious allergic reaction that affects the whole body and may cause breathing difficulties, fainting, or even death if not treated promptly.

anti-inflammatory—a drug that reduces inflammation and swelling.

antibodies—proteins produced by white blood cells. Some antibodies help to kill germs.

antihistamine—a drug that stops the effects of histamine and, as a result, relieves allergy symptoms.

asthma—a disease in which the air passages in the lungs become inflamed, making breathing difficult. Asthma attacks may be caused by exposure to allergens.

blocking antibodies—IgG antibodies produced in response to allergy shots. They compete with IgE antibodies and tie up allergens so that an allergic reaction will not occur.

bronchodilator—a drug that opens the airways during an asthma attack.

dander—flakes of dead skin from animals. People may be allergic to the dander of certain animals.

decongestant—a drug that reduces swelling in the breathing passages.

dust—a powdery substance containing fibers from bed linens, flakes of dead skin, pollen grains, mold spores, insect parts, and dust mites.

dust mite—a microscopic animal that feeds on the flakes of dead skin in house dust. People may be allergic to dust mite droppings.

eczema—a type of allergic skin rash.

elimination diet—a method of testing for allergies. It involves stopping all suspected foods for a while, then trying them one at a time to see if an allergic reaction occurs.

epinephrine—a drug that helps to ease a severe allergic reaction.

hay fever—a seasonal allergy that produces sneezing and other cold-like symptoms due to a reaction to plant pollens.

histamine—a chemical released by mast cells that causes tissues to become inflamed.

hives—swollen, itchy bumps on the skin due to an allergic reaction.

IgE—the kind of antibodies involved in allergic reactions.

IgG—the main kind of antibodies produced against germs and foreign substances that get into the blood.

immune system—the body's disease-fighting system, including white blood cells.

inflammation—redness and swelling as a result of damage or an allergic reaction.

lactose intolerance—an inability to digest milk sugar (lactose), resulting in stomachache, gas, or diarrhea.

mast cell—a special cell in the skin and the lining tissues (such as in the breathing passages). Mast cells bind to IgE antibodies and release histamine and other inflammation chemicals.

mast cell stabilizer—a drug such as Nasalcrom (cromolyn) that stops mast cells from releasing histamine.

mold—a fungus that grows on rotting plant or animal matter. People may be allergic to the tiny spores that molds send into the air to reproduce.

mucus—a slimy fluid that lines breathing passages.

parasite—a living thing that feeds on another living thing.

patch test—a skin test used to check for allergies to things that people touch, such as poison ivy.

poison ivy—a common plant that produces oils to which most people are allergic.

pollen—a powdery substance produced by flowers. It contains the plant's male sex cells.

ragweed—a common plant to which many people are allergic. It produces its pollen in late summer.

RAST test—a blood test for specific kinds of IgE antibodies to show sensitivity to particular allergens.

RIST test—a blood test that measures the amount of IgE in the blood.

scratch test—an allergy test in which a tiny bit of allergen is placed on a scratch to see if a skin reaction occurs.

sensitization—development of an allergy after repeated exposure to an allergen.

spores—seedlike cells released by fungi.

white blood cells—blood cells that can move through tissues and are an important part of the body's defenses. Some white blood cells eat germs and clean up bits of damaged cells and dirt.

Learning More

Books

Barbara Mitchell, *Zooallergy: A Fun Story About Allergy and Asthma Triggers*, Valley Park, MO: JayJo Books, 1996.

William and Vivian Ostrow, *All About Asthma*, Morton Grove, IL: Albert Whitman & Co., 1993.

Susan Neiberg Terkel, *All About Allergies*, New York: Lodestar Books, 1993.

Elizabeth Weitzman, *Let's Talk About Having Allergies*, New York: Rosen Publishing Group, 1998.

Organizations and Online Sites

AIR—Allergy Internet Resources

http://www.io.com/allergy/allabc.html#general

This site links you to web sites with information about asthma, food allergies, kids' allergies, hay fever, skin allergies, and stings and anaphylactic shock.

Allergy, Asthma & Immunology Online

http://allergy.mcg.edu/

Learn about children's allergies, rhinitis, food allergies, house dust allergies, asthma, and "when you should see an allergist."

AllerDays

http:/www.allerdays.com/

This site has fun features for allergy sufferers. It was created and is maintained by Hoechst Marion Roussel, a company that makes and sells prescription medications.

American Academy of Allergy, Asthma and Immunology
611 East Wells Street
Milwaukee, WI 53202
http://www.aaaai.org/

American College of Allergy, Asthma & Immunology
85 West Algonquin Road, Suite 550
Arlington Heights, IL 60005

Food Allergy Network
10400 Eaton Place, Suite 107
Fairfax, VA 22030-2208

National Institute of Allergy and Infectious Diseases
National Institutes of Health
Bethesda, MD 20892

The Virtual Children's Hospital

http://www.vh.org/Patients/IHB/Peds/Allergy/Managing Allergies/

This site describes how to manage allergies at school.

Index

Page numbers in *italics* indicate illustrations.

About the Authors

Dr. Alvin Silverstein is a Professor of Biology at the College of Staten Island of the City University of New York. **Virginia Silverstein** is a translator of Russian scientific literature. The Silversteins first worked together on a research project at the University of Pennsylvania. Since then, they have produced six children and more than 150 published books for young people.

Laura Silverstein Nunn, a graduate of Kean College, has been helping with her parents' books since her high school days. She is the coauthor of more than twenty books on diseases and health, science concepts, endangered species, and pets. Laura lives with her husband Matt and their young son Cory in a rural New Jersey town not far from her childhood home.